BEING ME IS ENOUGH

For Women

Lisa V. Taitt-Stevenson

DEDICATION

To my circle of sisters who refused to allow me to rest in a place of mediocrity and continue to this day to push me to strive for greatness. I am bits and pieces of each of you. I couldn't be where I am today without you all. Thank you for believing in me so much that I began to believe in myself.

We tend to discount the various roles we have by proclaiming that "I am just a…". You weren't "just" created to be "just a" anything. Own who you are and shout it out to the world boldly, proudly, and unapologetically.

ACKNOWLEDGMENTS

To all the women who have at one time or another questioned their worth; you are invaluable. To the woman that needs reminding of the greatness that resides within her; you are exceptional.

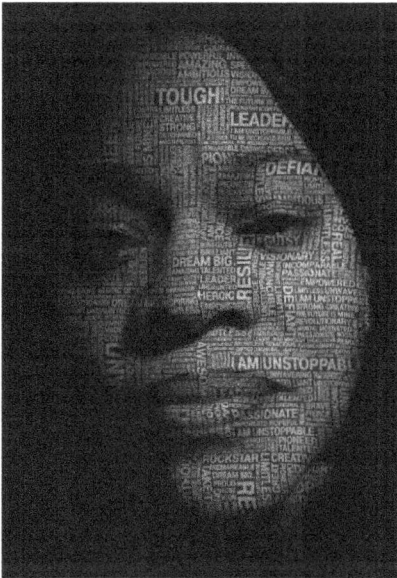

To the woman who goes through life loving everyone else first and barely having enough time to acknowledge herself; you are beyond compare. To the woman who allows life to define her from day to day; you are unparalleled. Let us never forget who we are, we encompass all of these amazing things and more...WE ARE WOMEN.

BEING ME IS ENOUGH

For Women

1

I am a Warrior. As I stand here unwavering in my womanhood, I stand unflinching in my purpose.

2

Today I will embrace my inner child and color outside of the lines; some lines are meant to be crossed.

3

I give myself permission to be happy and enjoy life.

4

My scars don't lessen my worth, they increase my value.

5

We are all consistent even in our inconsistencies; the key is to be consistent where it counts.

6

Some work within the box, some work outside of the box; I choose to work as if there is no box.

7

I will not walk into tomorrow with today's baggage.

8

I will Always be more than enough!

9

I am not defined by my circumstances, my definition comes from how I rise above them.

10

I Respect Myself

11

...because I deserve Respect!

12

I will no longer live in the world of "What if" but stand in the land of "I did".

13

I am Grateful!

14

I will not wait on others to set my goals. I choose to take control of my destiny and decide for myself.

15

I shall be heard.

16

I am Beautiful!

17

I am not Invisible, I am Invincible.

18

I am ready for success and I get to decide what that success looks like.

19

I am loved...from the sweet kiss of the sun on my face, to the good morning neighborly greeting, I am loved.

From the opening of the building door, to the holding of the elevator, I am loved.

From the glow of the moon shining through my bedroom window, to the cool pillow where I lay my head to go to sleep, I am loved.

In all things, I am loved.

20

I will not live in fear, at least not the kind that will keep me at a standstill. I will use my fears to propel me into the future I want.

21

I love the skin that I am in.

22

*I will live my life
with Intention;
Intentional
thoughts.
Intentional actions.*

23

I am not afraid of challenges; the trials of today will be the victories of tomorrow.

24

*I am determined.
Determined to be,
live, love, and inspire.*

25

I know who I am.

I am a mother, a wife, a friend, a boss, a leader, a nurturer, a counselor, a mentor...I know who I am.

26

It's time for
"W.I.N.E."

Winning, Innovation,
Networking, and
Engaging.

27

I am in charge of my emotions, my words, my fears, and my story.

28

I recognize my happiness starts and ends with me.

29

I own my truth.

30

I won't allow myself to get distracted by... Wait, is it nap time yet?

31

I will not settle for anything less than the expectations that I set for myself.

32

I am selfless; I will continue to give of myself, but not to the detriment of myself.

33

*I will dare to be bold;
Bold in my wants,
needs, desires, and
goals.*

34

In all things, I will honor myself; recognizing how I treat myself dictates how others will treat me.

35

I am a Strong Woman!

36

I will not conform to the world's perception of what I should be, because being uniquely me is More Than Enough.

37

I am Powerful!

38

I will no longer hold onto things that no longer serve a purpose in my life.

39

Despite the heartache and heartbreak, I still have an incredibly loving heart.

40

$$\approx\!\!\gg$$

*Today I will
intentionally empower
another woman.*

41

I am committed to sharing my journey so the ones behind me can learn from my missteps.

42

I will never stop
working on me
because I am worth
the investment.

43

Being a winner doesn't have a time frame; Whether it takes a week, a month, or a year to accomplish my goal(s), I am Still a Winner.

44

I am inspired by my everyday encounters. The birds inspire me to not only rely on my own merit to rise above the clouds, but to allow other factors to assist me. Motivation from friends, assistance from associates, guidance from family and determination from the doubt of the naysayers.

45

I wear many hats and I wear them well. Some hats I chose, and others were given. Regardless of how I got them, they are mine, and I wear them to the best of my ability.

46

I can move mountains! It is the audacity of my words that will move mountains; the boldness of my statements, and the conviction of my tone.

47

I am more than what the world sees. What may be seen as selfish is actually self-preservation. What may be perceived as weak, is actually silent strength. What may be viewed as tears of sadness, are actually tears of joy; because what I've been through has brought me to this breakthrough.

48

I am not just my body. I am the spirit that nurtures one's soul. I am the mind that navigates the waters of life painstakingly. I am the words that guides and advises without hesitation. I am not just my body.

49

Today I will keep my head in the clouds because there is no limit to how far my dreams can go.

50

I forgive myself for my Past, Present, and Future mistakes.

51

I am worth it. Time was taken to create me. Time was taken to develop me. Time is taken to understand me. I am worth it.

52

I am deserving of ALL
that life has to offer,
whether I take it or
not, is up to me.
Every morning I wake
with the opportunity
to choose what life is
offering.

53

I will not dim my light just so others can shine.

54

I am joy. I have the ability to be joy, create joy, bring joy, show joy, sit with joy, stand with joy, cry with joy, and laugh with joy. In all things I experience joy.

55

I am in love with me!

56

Today I will boldly and humbly walk in my greatness.

57

I have the ability to empower others. My life, my walk, my journey. My smile despite the pain, my courage despite the fear, my ability to rise day after day empowers.

58

I am not afraid to stand for what is right, and as much effort as I put into standing up for others, I will put into standing up for myself.

59

Regardless of how many times I fall, I will always rise.

60

I am forever changing, growing, and evolving.

61

I am thoughtful with my words; I will not speak just for the sake of speaking.

62

I will remind myself daily that I am never alone. Someone, somewhere, has walked the path that I am walking.

63

I am an entrepreneur. Whether it is in the way I organize my home, manage my family, balance my budget, or run my business, I am a boss.

64

The root of my unhappiness is the misconception that my happiness comes from everyone else but me.

65

I am thankful for each and every one of my relationships; they either show me what I want or don't want in my life.

66

I will build my team to help me get to the next level, understanding that my team may not consist of my inner circle.

67

People are in my life for many different reasons, it is up to me to take the time to determine what purpose each person serves.

68

I have a voice and I will use it. I will no longer allow fear to keep me from declaring my wants and needs.

69

I am a woman with a story. A story that holds no shame, guilt or judgment. It's my story.

70

Through the failures, the distractions, and the setbacks, I will stay on my grind.

71

My life is worth living!

72

I love naps….Is it nap time yet?

73

Life is like a pair of bell bottom pants, it all comes back around.

74

Today I will keep my opinion to myself until someone asks me for it, then I will let the good times roll. (just kidding...not really...ok, yes, I am kidding...maybe. (LOL)

75

*I am an active
participant in my
success from planning
to profit.*

76

*When in doubt eat
Jell-O.*

77

I can see all things clearly...when I put my glasses on; remove the preconceived notions, the assumptions, and the judgment, and just look at it for what it is.

78

I will not say I
understand when I do
not, or when I do not
want to.

79

Being Me Will Always Be Enough!

80

I am encouraged. Every day the sun and the moon do their job. In between is my opportunity to do mine.

81

Today I will strive to be better than I was yesterday.

82

Self-love begins with self-talk. What are you saying? More importantly, what are you hearing?

83

While taking the time to work on someone else's dreams, I will always take time to work on my own. The energy I use to carry me through the day for their dream is a mere portion of what I have in reserve to achieve my own.

84

I will not always walk around the corner to cross the street; The scenic route doesn't need to be taken in everything I do.

85

I get to choose for me. At the end of the day why let someone else choose? I am the one that has to live with it.

86

Karma has the innate ability to tell me if I am the "ish" or if I ain't "ish".

87

If I am not where I want to be in life, I can change it. I am in control of my destiny.

88

When I rest my head at night it is my goal to be at peace with the decisions I have made throughout the day.

89

Naps make me smile...Is it nap time yet?

90

I will no longer be afraid of silence; there is no need to fear my own thoughts…I have the ability to control them.

91

I am an original; one of a kind. No one laughs like me, smiles like me, talks like me, or walks like me. I am who I am all by myself. I am loving every part of the original me I am to be.

92

Today I will bite my tongue and not cuss anyone out, at least not before I have my coffee (LOL).

93

I have my own talents and gifts. As I admire others, I will consider that one person's gifts DO NOT equate to my lack of talent or my inability to do something. When I find myself doubting my own abilities, I will change my view.

94

I will no longer sit in a cage of unforgiveness unnecessarily; I realize my forgiveness is not a pass for the person that hurt me, but a release from the pain so I can leave it in my past.

95

When standing at a fork in the road, before going left or right, I will ask myself why? Why this over that? Why that road over the other? Am I choosing out of fear or am I choosing despite fear?

96

I will consider that as we grow, so should our surroundings. So today, I will intentionally create the space that is tailored towards who I am choosing to be.

97

I am not a sore loser,
I just like winning
more.

98

I am unforgettable. Whether it's a good vibe or bad vibe. Whatever space I leave, I leave something. I am choosing to leave something that is worth remembering. A warm smile, an encouraging word, an inspirational story, a calming spirit, or a good laugh. Whatever "it" is, I choose. I will choose with intention and I will choose wisely.

99

If I am hungry, I will eat; If I am not, I won't. Everything in life should be this easy.

100

I am a Conqueror. Life will come at me at times with some "stuff". All that I have endured, weathered and walked, has prepared me for these moments. Those moments/times have shown me my strength and resilience. If I got through that, I can get through this. I Am A Conqueror!

101

Tomorrow morning I will stay in bed for an extra 5 minutes just to take in the gift of another day.

102

$$\approx\!\!\!\approx$$

I am an Extraordinary Woman!

103

*The only competition
I face daily is with
myself. Comparison
to others only sets me
up for a failure.*

104

I am in the zone and nothing is going to throw me off course.

105

I am not afraid to be loved by others. More importantly, I am not afraid to be loved by me. Loving myself means that I accept myself in all of my humanness.

106

I embrace change; change is good, change is great, change is necessary. Change can be scary, but nothing is more scary than standing still. When the fire is building or when the lion is approaching...MOVE!

107

When I look in the mirror, it is my goal to know who is staring back at me. Today I will begin to peel away the layers that either no longer belong to me or never did. Then I will get reacquainted with who I am, so when I look in the mirror again, I can honestly say that I love who is staring back at me.

108

I am not afraid to be seen because I am in control of how much the world sees.

109

Just because no one else is moving doesn't mean that I will lose momentum.

110

When loving you forces me to question the love I have for myself, I have to love you from afar.

111

My silence can be just as powerful as my voice.

112

All of this intentional affirming, motivating, and validating is wearing me out...Is it nap time yet?

113

I am not afraid of success in any capacity, love, career, peace, or family life. I choose to rise above the bar and no longer fly just under the radar to ensure I do enough to not get noticed and not too little to get called out. My success doesn't just affect me.

114

I can and will be my own cheerleader; I will cheer so loudly that my naysayers will have no choice but to cheer along with me.

115

I acknowledge my inner beauty – exterior beauty fades, but the beauty I have within me is timeless and limitless. I am a true, natural beauty.

116

Today I will get out of "auto-pilot" mode and move with intention. I will no longer do drive by greetings; I will stop and be present to the conversations I start or have been invited into.

117

I am a Fighter!

118

I am not a quitter!

119

*I choose to use words
that are uplifting.*

120

I am loved, liked, admired, acknowledged, and embraced despite my flaws.

121

Every conflicting moment has the opportunity to be an educating moment.

122

I am who I choose to be.

123

I am a rare and beautiful gem.

124

I am not a doormat; I will not allow myself to be walked all over!

125

Instead of "why me?" being the default response, I will work from the "why not me?" response.

126

I am stronger than I know. When I look back over my life, I can honestly say, "It didn't break me. I am still standing".

127

I am Important!

128

Today I choose to be happy, while looking for happiness in every situation.

129

I will make time for me.

130

I am:

Unafraid!
Graceful!
Powerful!
A Visionary!
Prosperous!
Limitless!
Purposeful!
I am a Woman!!!

131

I can make a difference; I will no longer underestimate my role in this world.

132

I will operate in love – Operating in love doesn't mean everything you do will be warm and fuzzy. What it does mean, is that in all things you are mindful of the motivation behind the movement. Are your words malicious? Are your thoughts self-deprecating? Are your steps destructive? So now, "Ask yourself, "Are you operating in love?"

133

I have greatness within me!

134

※

I will start taking my own advice; clearly I know what I am talking about if people keep coming to me, so why not listen to what I have to say?

135

I am patient; the key
is learning to be
patient with myself.

136

My feelings matter.

137

I am a day dreamer, night dreamer, and in between dreamer.

138

I represent light.

139

Tonight, before I go to sleep, I will make bed angels.

140

Pity parties don't
need any more guests.
When faced with an
invitation I will
politely decline.

141

I am open to all possibilities.

142

I will take note of my breath today and as I inhale life, I will exhale negativity.

143

I will no longer live my life on the sidelines, I will get on the court and get involved.

144

I will no longer underestimate my ability to be become the woman I say I want to be.

145

I am so funny, I laugh harder at my own jokes than anyone else does.

146

Today, every time I walk passed a mirror, I will say, "Hello Gorgeous"...because I am.

147

I can't control how I am perceived but, I can control how I am presented.

148

I am determined to
accomplish my goals.

149

I am not defined by others' opinions of me.

150

It's never too late to start making smart choices.

151

I am a producer; I can and will get it done.

152

Today I choose to be productive rather than busy.

153

I live with Purpose, on Purpose, for a Purpose.

154

I love myself...flaws and all.

155

I may cry, I may scream, I may even cuss but, I will never give up!

156

I love me some me!

157

*I am not afraid, to be
the me that I am to be.*

158

Yes, I am that chick!

159

I will not discount the progress I have made so far just because I am not as close to my goal(s) as I would like to be.

160

My desire for my future is greater than the pain of my past.

161

I will acknowledge someone's potential while never losing sight of their patterns.

162

Today I will sit down and listen to what is and isn't being said.

163

I will no longer stand in a 2nd place slot and expect 1st place treatment.

164

As I move throughout the day I will ensure my actions line up with my words. Am I saying one thing but doing another?

165

My success is what I deem it to be; No one can tell me what my success should look like except for me.

166

Regardless of how long my dream remains dormant, I still have the ability to resurrect it, and fulfill that dream.

167

Today If I get ticked off, I will pause, take a breath, calm down, and cuss them out with a clear head, no need to get my thoughts all jumbled up because other people are acting a fool.

168

My life has meaning, so while I am reminding someone else of their value, I will continue to do the same for myself.

169

The time for wine is NOW...and then again tomorrow and the day after that.

170

I am Authentic!

171

I am a Woman of Substance!

172

Every day I will take
the time to
acknowledge who I
am to myself.

173

I have the power to make an impact on the world.

174

I acknowledge that
my opinion is mine
and if no one has
asked me for it, then
with me is where it
will stay.

175

I will remember to take my moment to refuel.

176

I will be unapologetic
in my success.

177

I will not be afraid to live My life, My way.

178

I am loving all of me today and to ensure I feel the same way tomorrow, I will read this again tomorrow.

179

I am strong. Despite my fears, I continue to push forward.

180

I will remember to celebrate my small victories.

181

I will no longer excuse my way out of opportunities.

182

My past is not a resting stop, it's a guiding post.

183

A No to chaos is a Yes to my inner peace.

184

I am not afraid of
being vulnerable with
the one who deserves
my vulnerability.

185

I am Confident!

186

Today, I will remember to tell myself, "I love you!"

187

It's never too late to be who I want to be.

188

Being Me Is truly Enough!

189

I am worth the fight; there are those that will fight for me and lend their voice for me, but there will be times that I must be at the head of that fight.

190

I am not afraid to be transparent.

191

I am thankful; I am thankful for all that I have and the things that I no longer hold on to.

192

Today I will be Intentionally Intentional.

193

I reserve the right to be me.

194

Although someone else's dreams may ask me to compromise my integrity, my dreams never will.

195

Today I will consider that though it may appear the grass is greener on the other side, there is also the possibility that there is no grass on the other side at all.

196

There is a place for everything in my home; love, peace, and joy. Anything that doesn't belong there; chaos, jealousy, or negativity, will be left outside.

197

When I fix my relationship with myself is when I can successfully cultivate my relationships with others.

198

I am Fearless!

199

I am a teacher. I will be mindful of my words and the seeds (or weeds) I plant using them.

200

I am Intelligent!

201

Rather than blame others for my decisions, I will focus on myself and being at peace with the decisions I have made until I can change them or fully accept them.

202

I will be courageous enough to keep moving.

203

I am More Than Enough!

204

I am far more than what the world sees; I will no longer be afraid to be great and show it.

205

I like myself.

206

Giving up is not an option.

207

I am proud of who I am.

208

I may not love everything but I am open to liking most things.

209

Everyone has a choice; Now consider, not choosing is a choice.

210

Dear Worry,
    I have to break up with you. I have been in this <u>relationship</u> way too long.

Sincerely,
Me

211

Rather than be envious of what my sisters have, I will admire and acknowledge their strengths.

212

Before I get down on myself, I will take note of how far I have come.

213

I won't focus on the speed of my movements; all that matters is that I keep moving forward.

214

I choose to believe in
the impossible.

215

Opportunities or Obstacles; my perspective will decide which one I see.

216

I have the ability to
decide.

217

Before I react, I will take a peak behind the curtain. There may be more going on than I realize and it may not even be about me.

218

⚭

I will either live in my fears or my dreams, I can't do both.

219

Today I choose
happiness over
sadness.

220

I choose to remain in a state of gratitude and joy.

221

Just for a moment I will take the time to simply breathe and take it all in.

222

Inner Peace is my New Success.

223

Tomorrow will forever remain tomorrow until I say today.

224

I may not like all of my decisions but I will own them.

225

I no longer have to choose between This or That; I can have This and That.

226

I will love life and
allow life to love me
back.

227

I can accomplish anything I set my mind to.

228

*I recognize that the
real me is better than
the fake them.*

229

I am Fierce!

230

I am forgiving of myself.

231

I will work on creating a life I can love, until then, I will continue to appreciate all that I have.

232

Some discomfort is meant to send you in another direction, and some are meant to mold you, shape you, and prepare you.

233

Road rage is real...Today I will try not to hit anyone with my car. LOL

234

Today I will put in the extra effort to wear matching socks. LOL

235

I can face any obstacle.

236

I am an extraordinary human being.

237

I will no longer block my blessings.

238

From this day forward, I will live without judgement; judgement from others and judgement from myself.

239

I Love My Body.

240

I will Always Be More Than Enough!

241

The decisions I make don't define me, it's what I do with those decisions after.

242

I am responsible for
my thoughts and
actions.

243

I will allow myself to make mistakes because it means that I have at least tried.

244

*I stand in my truth
unapologetically.*

245

Wherever I am at any given moment I will be present.

246

I choose to live my life on my own terms.

247

I am:

Courageous!
Innovative!
Bold!
Resilient!
Humble!
Fearless!
Driven!
I am a Woman!!!

248

I am not afraid to be who I am.

249

Today I will say yes to something new.

250

Today I will acknowledge the fact that I add value to the lives of those around me.

251

Today I will celebrate my existence.

252

Every morning I wake is a reminder that all things are possible.

253

I Believe In Myself.

254

I do not have to be
right all the time;
sometimes the greater
victory comes after
the misstep.

255

I am a SHE-ro to many people including myself.

256

I will take the time to
be proud of my
achievements.

257

I will walk with my head held high.

258

As I receive opportunities presented to me, I will create opportunities for those around me.

259

As I leave home today, I will take a moment to feel the warmth of the sun on my face.

260

As I strive to reach my goals, I will remember to call on others to help me along the way.

261

*Today is going to be
an Intentionally
Amazing day!*

262

I will take time to listen to what my body is telling me.

263

Today, I will take myself out on a date.

264

I am a woman with integrity.

265

I deserve all the wonderful things that life has to offer.

266

I will face my
challenges and
conquer them.

267

I will not only wait for holidays to celebrate me.

268

I will not allow my past to hold me captive; I've taken up residency there for far too long.

269

My goal is to continue moving forward regardless of who's coming with me or not.

270

I am Victorious!

271

The walls I keep around me to "protect" me aren't just keeping out the hurt, they are also keeping out the gifts that life brings and the love I am meant to share in.

272

Though I may lie to others, I will not lie to myself. (there really is no need, I can always tell)

273

I truly believe I can do anything I dedicate myself to; the problem is, I don't want to do everything I "dedicate" myself to. Now comes the question, how bad do I want it?

274

What was meant to harm me, strengthens me.

275

Every mistake is a lesson learned.

276

My goal is to be relevant while I am here and long after I am gone. I am building a legacy.

277

I am Beautiful!

278

I am Powerful!

279

It's one thing when I waste my time, it's another when I allow someone else to waste my time.

280

I love my face; the face that is staring back at me when the mask comes off.

281

I Love Who I am.

282

I am Brave!

283

When I come in from the rain, I will not hide my umbrella. Instead I will take the time to tell the next person it's raining outside.

284

When all else fails, I will rest in the fact that it is what it is until it isn't.

285

I will never give up on my dreams; my "why?" is what motivates me.

286

Every day I have the
ability to take my
power back.

287

I am present. Present to all that is within me and all that is around me.

288

Every morning I wake with a destiny. Will my actions today push me toward it or will I avoid it at all costs?

289

Today I will savor every "meal" and relish every bite given through, food, wisdom, and love.

290

When I stop enjoying the sound of my own voice, I know it's time to stop talking.

291

I am Royalty!

292

I have already mastered my patterns, now I will work diligently towards my potential.

293

I am Forever Blessed.

294

Who I was yesterday
is not who I am today
nor who I will be
tomorrow. I will enjoy
the journey while
remaining present to
the moments.

295

The love I give knows no boundaries. I love passed the pain, passed the hurt, passed the disappointments.

296

I am ready for the right kind of love, first from myself and then from others. The kind of love that doesn't hurt but comforts, doesn't tear down but uplifts, doesn't belittle but inspires.

297

I am a QUEEN!

298

I will **always** be **more** than enough!

ABOUT THE AUTHOR

Everyone has their inner battles, the ones that no one sees. I grew up in Bed Stuy, Brooklyn with a love for dance and music. They were my voice and helped me overcome insurmountable obstacles. From the age of four I learned to be a warrior. My inner child is my engine, and her resilience continues to push me to levels I didn't think were possible ...

During the time of the infamous 9-11 attack on the Twin Towers, I was once again called upon to rely on this resilience when I narrowly escaped the imploding buildings, and I was left to bear the weight of survivor's guilt. I vowed to help others and I rallied to summon my inner warrior as a pledge and a torch bearer. These words are the distillation of the inner wisdom of my soul. From my table to yours with love. I do not write anything that does not inspire or empower. I invite you to connect with passion and not just with pitfalls, and above all celebrate your triumphs!

Instagram: Authentic_Author911
E-mail: lwi.ltaitt@gmail.com

9 781733 525534